30 RADIO FAVORITES
THEN AND NOW

pg 134-139

3-19-02
$14.95

ISBN 1-57560-477-9

Copyright © 2001 Cherry Lane Music Company
International Copyright Secured   All Rights Reserved

Visit our website at www.cherrylane.com

CONTENTS

4	AGAIN	LENNY KRAVITZ
7	AMAZED	LONESTAR
12	BACK HERE	BBMAK
18	COLD AS ICE	FOREIGNER
22	CONVICTION OF THE HEART	KENNY LOGGINS
32	COUSIN DUPREE	STEELY DAN
36	DESERT ROSE	STING
44	DON'T SAY YOU LOVE ME	M2M
52	FROM A DISTANCE	BETTE MIDLER
57	HANGING BY A MOMENT	LIFEHOUSE
62	HUNGRY EYES	ERIC CARMEN
72	I HOPE YOU DANCE	LEE ANN WOMACK
80	I'M EVERY WOMAN	WHITNEY HOUSTON
67	JUST THE TWO OF US	WILL SMITH
88	LIQUID DREAMS	O-TOWN
92	MAGIC MAN	HEART
98	MISSING YOU	CASE
101	MMM BOP	HANSON
108	PIANO MAN	BILLY JOEL
118	SO VERY HARD TO GO	TOWER OF POWER
113	SOLID	ASHFORD & SIMPSON
122	SOMEDAY OUT OF THE BLUE (Theme from *El Dorado*)	ELTON JOHN
128	SUPERSTAR	THE CARPENTERS
130	THESE EYES	THE GUESS WHO
134	THIS MASQUERADE	GEORGE BENSON
140	(I'VE HAD) THE TIME OF MY LIFE	BILL MEDLEY & JENNIFER WARNES
150	WHAT A GIRL WANTS	CHRISTINA AGUILERA
158	WHEN YOU BELIEVE (from *The Prince of Egypt*)	WHITNEY HOUSTON AND MARIAH CAREY
172	WHERE IS THE LOVE?	ROBERTA FLACK
165	WIDE OPEN SPACES	DIXIE CHICKS

Again

Words and Music by
Lenny Kravitz

Amazed

Moderately slow Country Ballad

Words and Music by
Chris Lindsey, Marv Green
and Aimee Mayo

with pedal

Ev - 'ry time our eyes meet, this feel - in' in - side me
The smell of your skin, the taste of your kiss,

is al - most more— than I— can take.—
the way you whis - per in— the dark.—

*Recorded a half step lower.

baby, I'm a-mazed by you.

baby, I'm a-mazed by you.

Ev-'ry lit-tle thing that you do.

I'm so in love with you. It just keeps get-tin' bet - ter.

I wan-na spend the rest of my life_____ with you by my side_____

_____ for-ev-er and__ ev - er.   Ev - 'ry lit - tle thing that you do,__

_____ oh,_____ ev-'ry lit - tle thing that you__ do,__

Freely   **Tempo I**

Tacet

_____ ba-by, I'm a - mazed__ by__ you.

mp   *rit.*

Back Here

Words and Music by Christian Burns,
Mark Barry, Stephen McNally
and Phil Thornalley

Moderate Rock

Ba - by, set me free ___ from this mi - ser - y. ___ I can't take it no more. ___
So I told you lies, ___ e - ven made you cry. ___ Ba - by, I was so wrong. ___

Since you ran a - way ___ noth - in's been the same. Don't
Girl, I prom - ise you ___ now my love is true. This ___

___ know what I'm liv - in' for. ___ Here I am, ___ so a - lone ___
___ is where my heart be - longs. ___

and there's noth - ing in this world I can do _____ un - til you're

back here _ ba - by. _____ Miss _ you, want _ you, need_

_ you so un - til you're back here _ ba - by, yeah. _ There's a

feel - in' in - side I want _ you to know. You are the one _ and I can't_

so a - lone, _____ and there's noth - in' in this world I can do. _____

Un - til you're back here _____ ba - by. _____

Miss _____ you, want _____ you, need _____ you so un - til you're

Cold As Ice

Words and Music by
Mick Jones and Lou Gramm

Some-day you'll __ pay the price, I know. I've

seen it be-fore; __ it hap-pens all the time. __ You're clos-ing the door; __ you leave the

world be-hind. __ You're dig-ging for gold __ yet throw-ing a-way __ a

for-tune in feel - ings, but some - day you'll pay.

19

some-day you'll pay.

Cold   as

Conviction of the Heart

Words and Music by
Guy Thomas and Kenny Loggins

(Instrumental)

Where are the dreams that we once had?
And down your streets I've walked a - lone,
It's been too man - y years of tak -ing now,

This is the
as if my
is - n't it

time to bring them back.
feet were not my own.
time to stop some - how?

What were the prom - is - es
Such is the path I chose,
Air that's too an - gry to breath,

One child, one dream, on - ly one life.
heart. With the earth, with the sky, one with

Give her one chance for one life.
ev - ery - thing in life. I be - lieve it will

When will we live?
start with con - vic - tion of the heart. With the

On - ly one earth, on - ly

one sky, on -ly one world. We've on -ly got one chance to live_ in
sky, with_ the_ earth, one_ with ev - ery - thing in

one life. I be - lieve_____ it's on - na start when we be-
life. I_ be - lieve it_ will_ start with_ con -

Bb Ebsus2   Ebmaj9 F

gin with some con - vic - tion of the heart.
vic - tion of the heart.

Bb Ebsus2   Ebmaj9 F Bb

Cousin Dupree

Words and Music by
Walter Becker and Donald Fagen

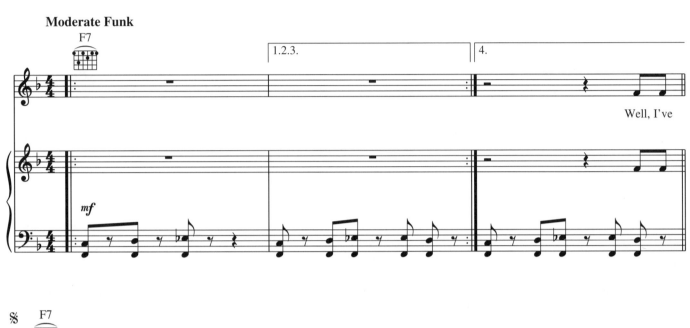

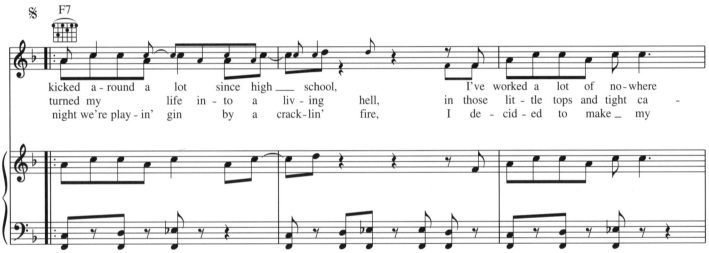

kicked a-round a lot since high __ school, I've worked a lot of no-where
turned my life in-to a liv-ing hell, in those lit-tle tops and tight ca -
night we're play-in' gin by a crack-lin' fire, I de-cid-ed to make __ my

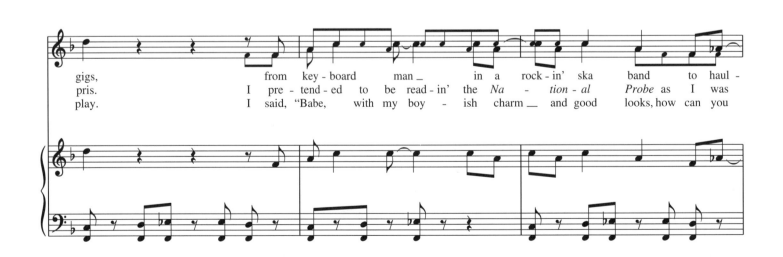

gigs, from key-board man __ in a rock-in' ska band to haul-
pris. I pre-tend-ed to be read-in' the *Na - tion - al Probe* as I was
play. I said, "Babe, with my boy-ish charm __ and good looks, how can you

Desert Rose

Written and Composed by
Sting

improvised arabic lyrics

3. And as she turns, e - lay,___ e - lay.___ This way she moves in the lo - - - gic of all my dreams. This fire___ burns, e - lay,___ e - lay.___ I re - al - ise that no - thing's as___ it seems.

D.S. al Coda

⊕ *Coda* Cm

Verse 4:
I dream of rain, elay, elay
I dream of gardens in the desert sand
I wake in pain, elay, elay
I dream of love as time runs through my hand.

Chorus 2:
I dream of rain, elay, elay
I lift my gaze to empty skies above
I close my eyes, her rare perfume
Is the sweet intoxication of her love.

Don't Say You Love Me

Words and Music by
Peter Zizzo, Jimmy Bralower,
Marion Elise Ravn and Marit Larsen

44

don't Don't say you love me, baby, baby.
Don't say you love me; you don't even know me. If

you really want me, then give me some time.
Give me some

time.

Don't say you love me; you don't even know me. If

From a Distance

Words and Music by
Julie Gold

dis - tance there___ is har - mo - ny, and it___
dis - tance we___ are in - stru- ments, march - ing___
dis - tance there___ is har - mo - ny, and it___

ech - oes through___ the land.___ It's the
in a com - mon band.___ Play - ing
ech - oes through___ the land.___ It's the

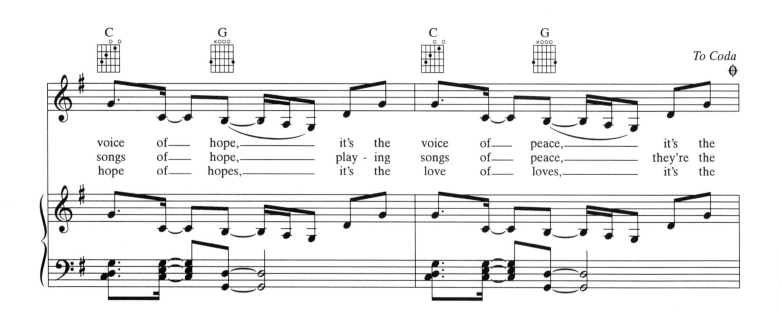

voice of___ hope,___ it's the voice of___ peace,___ it's the
songs of___ hope,___ play - ing songs of___ peace,___ they're the
hope of___ hopes,___ it's the love of___ loves,___ it's the

54

voice of ev - 'ry man.
songs of ev - 'ry

man.   God__ is watch-ing us,__ God__ is watch-ing us,   God__ is

From a

watch-ing us   from a dis-tance.__

Hanging by a Moment

Words and Music by
Jason Wade

Medium Rock

Des - p'rate ___ for chang - ing.
get - ting all ___ I'm lack - ing. Com -

Starv - ing ___ for truth. ___ I'm
plete - ly in - com - plete. ___ I'll

clos - er to where I start - ed.
take your in - vi - ta - tion.

* Recorded a half step lower.

* 2nd and 3rd times sing 8va (next 8 bars only)

Lyrics:
Chas - ing af - ter you. _____ I'm fall - ing e - ven
You take all _____ of me. _____

more in love _____ with you. _____ Let - ting go of all I've held _____ on - to. _____

_____ I'm stand - ing here un - til you make _____ me move. _____ I'm hang - ing by a

mo - ment here _____ with you. _____

58

For - I'm liv-ing for the

on - ly thing __ I know. __ I'm run-ning and not quite sure where __ to go. __

__ I don't know what I'm div-ing __ in - to. ___ Just hang-ing by a

To Coda

mo - ment here __ with you. __ There's noth-ing else to lose.

There's noth-ing else to find. _____ There's noth-ing in the

world that could change my mind. _____

There is noth-ing else. _____

There is noth-ing else.

Hungry Eyes

from the Vestron Motion Picture DIRTY DANCING

Words and Music by
Franke Previte and John DeNicola

Moderately fast

I've been mean-ing to tell ___ you

I've got this feel-ing that won't ___ sub - side.
I want to hold you, so hear ___ me out.

This love ____ was meant ____ to be. _____

(Sing 1st time only)

D.S. (take 2nd ending) and fade

I've got ____

Just the Two of Us

(Will Smith Rap)

Words and Music by
Ralph MacDonald, William Salter
and Bill Withers

Moderately

Guitar ——→ *Cmaj7* *B7* *Em* *Dm7* *G7*
(*capo 1st fret*)

Piano ——→ D♭maj7 C7 Fm E♭m7 A♭7

Cmaj7 *B7* *Em7* *Cmaj7* *B7♯5*

D♭maj7 C7 Fm7 D♭maj7 C7♯5

Em *Dm7* *G7* *Cmaj7* *B7♯5* *Em7*

Fm E♭m7 A♭7 D♭maj7 C7♯5 Fm7

Cmaj7 *B7* *Em* *Dm7* *G7*

D♭maj7 C7 Fm E♭m7 A♭7

I see the crys - tal rain - drops fall, and the beau - ty of it
We look for love; no time for tears. Wast - ed wa - ter's all that
I hear the crys - tal rain - drops fall on the win - dow down the

mf

all is when the sun comes shin-ing through___ to make those rain-bows in my
is, and it don't make no flow-ers grow.___ Good things might come to those who
hall, and it be-comes the morn-ing dew.___ And dar-ling, when the morn-ing

mind, when I think of you some - time, and I want to spend___ some time with
wait but not for those who wait too late. We've got to go___ for all we
comes and I see the morn - ing sun. I want to be___ the one with

you.___ Just___ the two of us, we can make it if___ we try.___ Just the
know.___
you.___

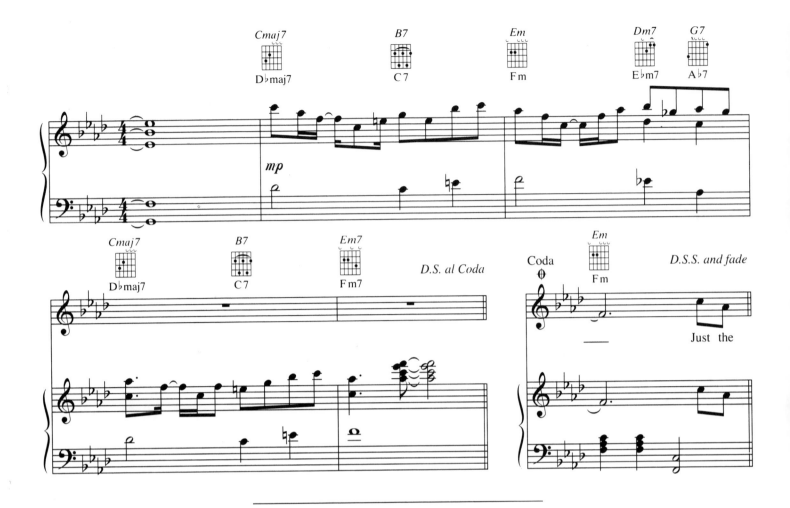

Just the Two of Us
Will Smith Rap

Words and Music by Ralph MacDonald, William Salter and Bill Withers

(Backing vocals:) Just the two of us. (5 times)

(Tre':)
Now Dad, this is a very sensitive subject.

From the first time the doctor placed you in my arms,
I knew I'd meet death 'fore I'd let you meet harm.
Although questions arose in my mind, would I be man enough?
Against wrong, choose right and be standin' up.
From the hospital that first night,
Took a hour just to get the car seat in right.
People drivin' all fast, got me kinda upset.
Gotcha home safe, placed you in your bassinet.
That night I don't think one wink I slept,
As I slipped out my bed, to your crib I crept.
Touched your head gently, felt my heart melt
'Cause I know I loved you more than life itself
Then to my knees, and I begged the Lord please,
Let me be a good daddy, all he needs
Love, knowledge, discipline, too,
I pledge my life to you.

(Will Smith Rap, cont.)

Chorus:
Just the two of us, we can make it if we try.
Just the two of us. (Just the two of us.)
Just the two of us, building castles in the sky.
Just the two of us, you and I.

Five years old, bringin' comedy.
Every time I look at you I think, man, a little me,
Just like me.
Wait and see, gonna be tall.
Makes me laugh 'cause you got your dad's ears an' all.
Sometimes I wonder what you gonna be.
A general? A doctor? Maybe a MC.
Ha, I wanna kiss you all the time,
But I will test that butt when you cut outta line, true that.
Uh-uh-uh, why you do dat?
I try to be a tough dad, but you be makin' me laugh.
Crazy joy when I see the eyes of my baby boy.
I pledge to you, I will always do everything I can,
Show you how to be a man.
Dignity, integrity, honor an'
I don't mind if you lose, long as you came with it.
And you can cry; ain't no shame in it.
It didn't work out with me an' your mom,
But yo, push come to shove,
You was conceived in love.
So if the world attacks and you slide off track,
Remember one fact, I gotcha back.

Repeat Chorus

It's a full-time job to be a good dad,
You got so much more stuff than I had.
I gotta study just to keep with the changin' times.
A Hundred One Dalmations on your CD-ROM.
See me, I'm tryin' to pretend I know
On my PC where that CD go.
But yo, ain't nothin' promised, one day I'll be gone.
Feel the strife, but trust life does go on.
But just in case, it's my place to impart
One day some girl's gonna break your heart.
And ooh, ain't no pain like from the opposite sex.
Gonna hurt bad, but don't take it out on the next, Son.
Throughout life people will make you mad,
Disrespect you and treat you bad.
Let God deal with the things they do,
'Cause hate in your heart will consume you, too.
Always tell the truth, say your prayers,
Hold doors, pull out chairs, easy on the swears.
You're living proof that dreams come true.
I love you and I'm here for you.

Repeat Chorus and fade

I Hope You Dance

Words and Music by Tia Sillers
and Mark D. Sanders

I hope you still __ feel small __ when you stand __ be-side _____ the
Don't let __ some hell - bent __ heart leave _____ you

o - cean.
bit - ter.
When-ev - er one __ door clos - es, I __
When you come close __ to sell - in' out, __

__ hope one __ more o - pens.
__ re - con - sid - er.
Prom - ise me __
Give the heav -

__ that you'll __ give faith _____ a fight - ing
- ens a - bove more _____ than just a pass - ing

79

I'm Every Woman

Words and Music by
Nickolas Ashford and Valerie Simpson

ly._____ 'Cause I'm_____ ev-ery wom - an, it's all in me._____

It's_ all in me,_____

yeah!

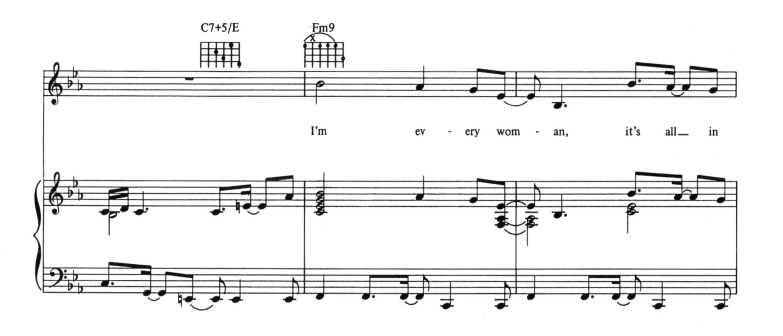

I'm ev - ery wom - an, it's all in

me.___ I can read your thoughts right now, ev - ery one from A___ to Z.___

I___

I'll do it nat - 'ral - ly.___

I'm ev - ery wom - an, it's all_ in

me.___ I can read your thoughts right now, ev - ery one from A__ to Z.__

86

Additional Lyrics

2. I can sense your needs like rain unto the seeds.
I can make a rhyme of confusion in your mind.
And when it comes down to some good old-fashioned love,
I've got it, I've got it, I've got it, got it, baby, 'cause...
(To Chorus)

Liquid Dreams

Words and Music by
Joshua P. Thompson, Bradley Spalter,
Michael Norfleet and Quincy Patrick

Magic Man

Words and Music by
Ann Wilson and Nancy Wilson

seen each oth - er in __ a dream.
tried to re - al - ize __ it all.

Seemed like he knew __ me. He
Ma - ma says she's wor - ried: grow-ing

looked right through __ me. __
up in a hur - ry. __

"Come on __ home, __ girl," he said with a smile. __
"Come on __ home, __ girl," Ma - ma cried on the phone. __ "Too

"You don't have to love __ me yet. Let's __ get high a - while. __ But
soon to lose my ba - by yet. My girl should be at home." __ But

Missing You

Words and Music by Joshua P. Thompson,
Tim Kelley, Bob Robinson
and Joe Thomas

like a wed - ding with-out a groom, ___ I'm miss - ing you. ___

I'm the des - ert with-out the sand. ___ You're the wom - an with-out a man. __

To Coda *2nd time, D.S. al Coda*

I'm the ring ___ with - out a hand. ___ I'm miss - ing ___ you. ___

4th time, D.S. and fade on Chorus
Play 4 times

Coda

I'm miss - ing ___ you. ___ Yeah, ___ yeah, ___ yeah, ___ yeah. __

100

MMM Bop

Words and Music by Isaac Hanson,
Taylor Hanson and Zac Hanson

ooh yeah. And they're gone___

___ so ___ fast.

So hold on to the ones who real - ly care; ___ in the end ___ they'll be the on - ly ones there. ___
Plant a seed; plant a flow - er; plant ___ a rose. ___ You can plant ___ an - y one of those. ___

___ When you get old ___ and start los - ing your hair, ___ can you tell me who ___ will ___
___ Keep plant - ing to find out which one grows. It's a se - cret no ___ one ___

Piano Man

Words and Music by
Billy Joel

mood for a mel - o - dy, and you've got us feel - in' al -

right. _____

Now
Now
It's a

Solid

Words and Music by
Nickolas Ashford and Valerie Simpson

* Tacet 1st time (play as written 2nd and 3rd times).

knew down the line ___ we would make it bet - ter.
love was so new; ___ we did what we had to. ___

And for love's ___ sake, ___ we were
And with that feel - ing, ___ we were

each mis - take, ___ oh, ___ you for - gave. ___
will - ing ___ to take a chance. ___

___ And soon ___ both of us ___
___ So a - gainst all odds, ___ we

So Very Hard to Go

Words and Music by
Stephen Kupka and Emilio Castillo

Ain't noth-in' I can say,_____ noth-in' I can
I knew the time would come_____ I'd have to pay for my mis-

do._____ I feel so bad,
takes._____ I can't blame you for what you're do-in' to me,

I feel so blue.
e-ven though my heart aches.

girl,

I got to make it right for ev-'ry-one con-cerned,
Your dreams have all come true, just the way you planned them.

3. *Instrumental*

e - ven if it's me, if it means it's a
So I'll just step a - side, I'm gon' step a -

me what's get-tin' burned.
side and lend a help-ing hand.

1.2.3. 'Cause I could nev - er

make_____ you un - hap - py.

No, I could-n't do that,

girl.___ On-ly wish I did-n't love you so;

makes it so ver - y hard to

go.___

(So ver - y hard to go.)

'Cause I love you so.___

(So ver - y hard to go.)

To Coda ⊕

1.

I___ love you so.___

Someday Out of the Blue

(Theme from El Dorado)
from THE ROAD TO EL DORADO

Lyrics by Tim Rice

Music by
Elton John and Patrick Leonard

123

*Guitarists: Slide capo to 4th fret.

Superstar

Words and Music by
Leon Russell and Bonnie Sheridan

These Eyes

Written by
Burton Cummings and Randy Bachman

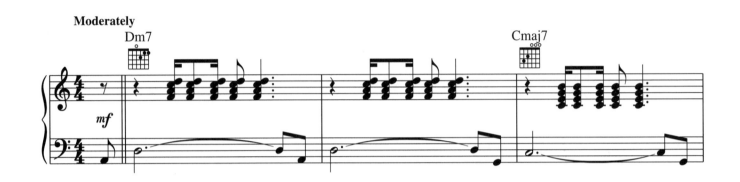

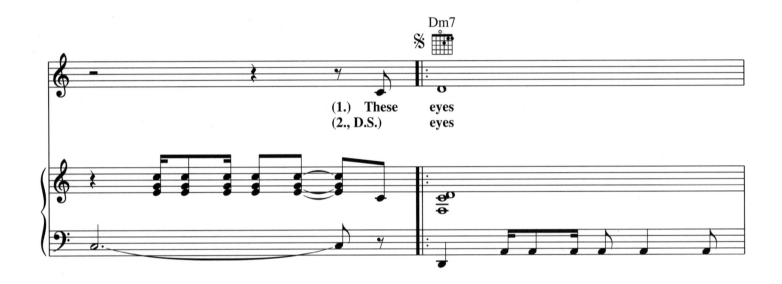

This Masquerade

Words and Music by
Leon Russell

*Guitar solo sounds 8va
lower than written.

quer - ade._____

(I've Had)
The Time of My Life

from DIRTY DANCING

Words and Music by
Franke Previte, John DeNicola,
and Donald Markowitz

owe it all to you.

Male: I've been wait-ing for so long; ___ now I've
fi-n'lly found some-one ___ to stand by me.

Female: We saw the
writ-ing on the wall ___ as we felt this mag-i-cal ___ fan-ta-

sy. _____

Both: Now with pas - sion in our eyes _____ there's no way we could _ dis - guise _____ it se - cret - ly. _____

So we take each oth-er's hand _____ 'cause we seem to un - der-stand _ the ur - gen -

cy.   *Male:* Just __ re - mem - ber,   *Female:* you're the

one thing   *Male:* I can't get e - nough __ of.   *Female:* So I'll tell you

some - thing: *Both:* this could be love.   Be - cause   I've __ had __

__ the time of my life. __   No, I nev - er felt __ this way be -

148

What a Girl Wants

Words and Music by Shelly Peiken
and Guy Roche

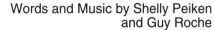

Moderately fast

What a girl wants, what a girl needs, what a girl wants, what a girl

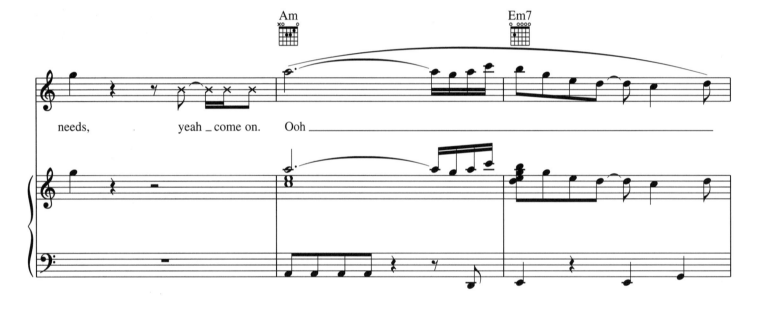

needs, yeah come on. Ooh

ah yeah. I wan-na thank you for giv-ing

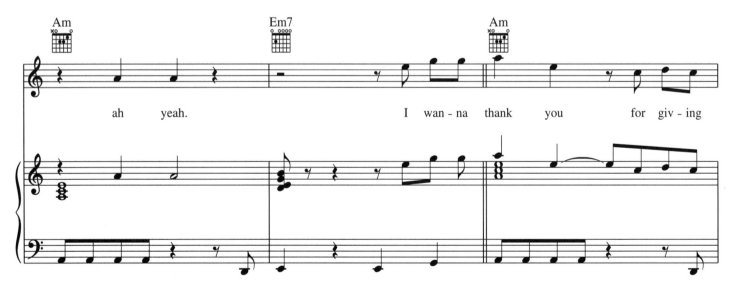

luck - y for me ___ you un - der - stand: ___ What a girl wants, (yeah) what a girl
needs (yeah) what-ev-er makes ___ me hap - py sets ___ you free. ___ And I'm
thank-ing you ___ for know-ing ex - act - ly what a girl wants, what a girl needs,
what - ev - er keeps ___ me in ___ your arms, ___ and I'm thank - ing you ___ for

When You Believe
(From The Prince of Egypt)

Words and Music Composed by Stephen Schwartz
with Additional Music by Babyface

Man-y nights we've prayed, with no proof an-y-one could hear.

In our hearts a hope-ful song— we bare-ly un-der-stood. Now

we are not— a-fraid, al-though we know there's much to fear.

You__ will__ when__ you__ be - lieve.__

They don't al - ways hap - pen when__ you ask.__

__ And it's eas - y to__ give in __ to your fear.__

__ But when__ you're blind - ed by__ your pain, can't see__

now   you will.   You will when you   be - lieve.

— You— will— when you, you will when   you——   be -

lieve,   just be - lieve,   just be -

lieve. You will when you   be - lieve.

Wide Open Spaces

Words and Music by
Susan Gibson

Who does-n't know what I'm talk-ing a - bout? _

Who's nev-er left home, who's _ nev-er struck out to find a

dream and a life __ of their own, a place __ in the clouds, _ a foun-da-

tion of stone? __

Man-y pre-cede and man-y will
She trav-eled this road __ as __ a

fol-low,
child, __

a young girl's dreams no long-er
wide-eyed and grin-ning, she nev-er

takes. She needs ___ new _____ fac-

es. She knows the high stakes. ___

stakes. ___ She know the high stakes. _____

Where Is the Love?

Words and Music by
Ralph MacDonald and William Salter

why   did   you   have   to___ lie?___
You've   got   to   let   me___ know.___
All   I   can   do   is___ wait.___

Do   do   do   do,___   do   do   do   do,

— do do do do___ do do___ do;   do do do do___

More Great Piano/Vocal Books from Cherry Lane

For a complete listing of Cherry Lane titles available, including contents listings, please visit our web site at
www.cherrylane.com

02500343	Almost Famous	$14.95
02501801	Amistad	$14.95
02502171	The Best of Boston	$17.95
02500144	Mary Chapin Carpenter – Party Doll and Other Favorites	$16.95
02502163	Mary Chapin Carpenter – Stones in the Road	$17.95
02502165	John Denver Anthology – Revised	$22.95
02505512	Best of John Denver for Easy Piano	$9.95
02503629	Best of John Denver – Piano Solos	$10.95
02502227	John Denver – A Celebration of Life	$14.95
02500002	John Denver Christmas	$14.95
02502166	John Denver's Greatest Hits	$17.95
02502151	John Denver – A Legacy in Song (Softcover)	$24.95
02502152	John Denver – A Legacy in Song (Hardcover)	$34.95
02500326	John Denver – The Wildlife Concert	$17.95
02509922	The Songs of Bob Dylan	$29.95
02500175	Linda Eder – It's No Secret Anymore	$14.95
02502209	Linda Eder – It's Time	$17.95
02509912	Erroll Garner Songbook, Vol. 1	$17.95
02500270	Gilbert & Sullivan for Easy Piano	$12.95
02500318	Gladiator	$12.95
02500273	Gold & Glory: The Road to El Dorado	$16.95
02502126	Best of Guns N' Roses	$17.95
02502072	Guns N' Roses – Selections from Use Your Illusion I and II	$17.95
02500014	Sir Roland Hanna Collection	$19.95
02502134	Best of Lenny Kravitz	$12.95
02500012	Lenny Kravitz – 5	$16.95
02502201	The Songs of David Mallett – A Collection	$17.95
02500003	Dave Matthews Band – Before These Crowded Streets	$17.95
02502199	Dave Matthews Band – Crash	$17.95
02502192	Dave Matthews Band – Under the Table and Dreaming	$17.95
02500081	Natalie Merchant – Ophelia	$14.95
02502204	The Best of Metallica	$17.95
02500010	Tom Paxton – The Honor of Your Company	$17.95
02507962	Peter, Paul & Mary – Holiday Concert	$17.95
02500145	Pokemon 2.B.A. Master	$12.95
02500026	The Prince of Egypt	$16.95
02502189	The Bonnie Raitt Collection	$22.95
02502230	Bonnie Raitt – Fundamental	$17.95
02502139	Bonnie Raitt – Longing in Their Hearts	$16.95
02502088	Bonnie Raitt – Luck of the Draw	$14.95
02507958	Bonnie Raitt – Nick of Time	$14.95
02502190	Bonnie Raitt – Road Tested	$24.95
02502218	Kenny Rogers – The Gift	$16.95
02500072	Saving Private Ryan	$14.95
02500197	SHeDAISY – The Whole SHeBANG	$14.95
02500166	Steely Dan – Anthology	$17.95
02500284	Steely Dan – Two Against Nature	$14.95
02500165	Best of Steely Dan	$14.95
02502132	Barbra Streisand – Back to Broadway	$19.95
02507969	Barbra Streisand – A Collection: Greatest Hits and More	$17.95
02502164	Barbra Streisand – The Concert	$22.95
02502228	Barbra Streisand – Higher Ground	$16.95
02500196	Barbra Streisand – A Love Like Ours	$16.95
02503617	John Tesh – Avalon	$15.95
02500128	Best of John Tesh (EZ Play Today)	$8.95
02502178	The John Tesh Collection	$17.95
02503623	John Tesh – A Family Christmas	$15.95
02505511	John Tesh – Favorites for Easy Piano	$12.95
02503630	John Tesh – Grand Passion	$15.95
02500124	John Tesh – One World	$14.95
02500307	John Tesh – Pure Movies 2	$14.95
02502175	Tower of Power – Silver Anniversary	$17.95
02502198	The "Weird Al" Yankovic Anthology	$17.95
02502217	Trisha Yearwood – A Collection of Hits	$16.95
02500334	Maury Yeston – December Songs	$17.95
02502225	The Maury Yeston Songbook	$19.95

See your local music dealer or contact:

CHERRY LANE MUSIC COMPANY
6 East 32nd Street, New York, NY 10016

EXCLUSIVELY DISTRIBUTED BY
HAL•LEONARD® CORPORATION
7777 W. BLUEMOUND RD. P.O. BOX 13819 MILWAUKEE, WI 53213

Prices, contents and availability subject to change without notice.